THE

K I D'S

GUIDE TO THE
GREAT SMOKY MOUNTAINS

Eileen Ogintz

Globe
Pequot

Guilford, Connecticut

Thank you to the National Park Service, the Great Smoky Mountains Association, Erin Evins, Heather Davis, Claire Ballentine, and Melanie Yemma for helping with the research for this book.

All the information in this guidebook is subject to change. We recommend that you call ahead to obtain current information before traveling.

Globe Pequot

An imprint of Rowman & Littlefield
Distributed by NATIONAL BOOK NETWORK
Copyright © 2016 by Eileen Ogintz

Illustrations licensed by Shutterstock.com and Thinkstock.com

British Library Cataloguing in Publication Information Available

Library of Congress Cataloging-in-Publication Data Available

ISBN 978-1-4930-2432-2 (paperback)
978-1-4930-2433-9 (e-book)

∞™ The paper used in this publication meets the minimum requirements of American National Standard for Information Sciences—Permanence of Paper for Printed Library Materials, ANSI/NISO Z39.48-1992.

Contents

1
Welcome to the Smokies!

Check out those mountains!

Do they look blue to you? The Cherokee described the Smoky Mountains as *shaconage*, meaning "blue, like smoke."

That's actually water vapor from all the rain in the peaks that in turn feeds all the amazing waterfalls and the streams where you can fish.

Welcome to Great Smoky Mountains National Park. Every national park is different and every one offers special adventures. At Great Smoky, there are adventures to be had all year long!

You can see a lot of the park from the car—pretty wildflowers, trees, the mountains, and maybe some historic

DID YOU KNOW?

People have occupied the Great Smoky Mountains since prehistoric times, but the first white settlers didn't arrive until the late 1700s and found they were on Cherokee land with permanent towns, political systems, and trails. Sadly, most of the Cherokee were forced to leave their home in the 1830s and relocate to Oklahoma. Many got sick and died along the way. The tragic episode is known as "The Trail of Tears." Those few who remained were the ancestors of the Cherokees who live near the park today. You might visit a museum on tribal lands in Cherokee, North Carolina, that helps preserve their history and culture.

buildings that will give you glimpses of what life would have been like for farm kids who lived here before this land was a national park.

But you will have so much more fun if you get out of the car to explore the huge park—at least some of it. The hardest part will be deciding what to do first:

- **TAKE A HIKE?** Maybe to a waterfall? There are over 800 miles of hiking trails from which to choose. Maybe you want to climb one of those mountain peaks?

- **GO ON A BIKE RIDE?** Especially on **Cades Cove Loop Road** when the road is closed to cars in summer.

- **HORSEBACK RIDE?**

- **FISH?** There are some 300 streams with plenty of fish. Have you ever caught a fish—and helped cook it for dinner?

- **GO CAMPING?** There are 10 **National Park Service campgrounds** from which to choose.

- **HAVE A PICNIC?** That's an especially good idea because there aren't a lot of restaurants here, but there are plenty of picnic areas.

- **APPRECIATE THE BEAUTY?** Count how many wildflowers you can see in the spring—there are more than 1,500 kinds of flowering plants here in spring and summer! Just don't pick any!

- **EXPLORE THE AREA'S HISTORY?** Learn what it was like for kids here by visiting an old schoolhouse, cabin, or other historic buildings. Kids only went to school in the winter, when they didn't have to help on the family farm.

- **LOOK FOR WILDLIFE?** You'll have the opportunity to observe many different animals, including black bear. Just don't get too close!

A LOCAL KID SAYS:
"I like to hike anywhere in the Smoky Mountains. It is all beautiful."
—Cody, 11, Greeneville, TN

■ **JOIN A RANGER** for a fun activity? Are you ready for **Animal Olympics** to see how you stack up next to the park's animals? Maybe you can learn how to use an old-fashioned loom, see a blacksmith work, or take a night hike under a full moon. Check out the special family programs when you arrive or online (nps.gov/grsm/index.htm).

The only hard part is deciding what you want to do first. Do you have your backpack ready?

DID YOU KNOW?

Great Smoky Mountains National Park was established in 1934 as a way to protect what remained of the mountains' forest from logging. Many land owners had to leave their land when the park was established and they left behind many buildings. Over 70 have been preserved so that Great Smoky Mountains National Park now contains the largest collection of historic log buildings in the East. You can visit some of them.

Bear Smarts

Biologists estimate that about 1,500 black bears live in the park. It's one of the largest protected areas in the eastern US where they can live in the wild. They are most active during the early morning and late evening in spring and summer. Park volunteers work hard to educate visitors about bears and caution you to be careful if you see a bear! A bear's behavior can be unpredictable. Always remember that bears in the park are wild, not like ones in a zoo.

Park officials say if you see a bear:

A VISITING KID SAYS:
"My favorite thing to do in the park was driving around looking for bears."
—Stephen, 12, Bristol, VA

- **DO NOT APPROACH** it and do not allow it to approach you.

- If the bear changes his behavior—starts watching you or stops feeding, for example—you are too close. Don't run, but back away slowly.

- If the bear keeps approaching you, change your direction. If the bear gets closer, talk loudly or shout. Act together as a group and make yourselves look as large as possible.

- Throw non-food objects toward the bear, such as rocks.

- Don't run or turn away.

- Don't leave food for the bear or any food where bears can get it. Human food changes the bears' behavior and causes them to lose their fear of humans. They can become more unpredictable. If the bear seems to be after your food, separate yourself from the food and slowly back away.

- Report the bear sighting as soon as possible to the park rangers.

DID YOU KNOW?

In the summer a typical adult male bear weighs about 250 pounds, but a female is less than half that. They will double their weight by the fall. Bear cubs weigh just a half pound when they are born.

TELL THE ADULTS

- There are more than 270 miles of road in the parks, and driving the mountains may be challenging if you aren't used to it.

- Keep extra distance between you and the vehicle in front of you!

- If your kids are prone to motion sickness, before you leave home, discuss with your pediatrician whether motion sickness medication is warranted and if so, give it to your child at least an hour before you anticipate being on mountainous roads.

A LOCAL KID SAYS:
"I've been to the park 25 times.
I like climbing on the rocks!"
—Sidney, 10, Knoxville, TN

- Avoid greasy or spicy meals the night before.

- Encourage the kids to drink plenty of water.

- Insist the kids put down their devices and look outside. Looking out at the horizon rather than down can also prevent motion sickness.

- Keep a stash of dry crackers, ginger ale, water, and ginger candies on hand. Ginger is a traditional remedy for nausea.

- Keep clean-up supplies handy—just in case.

DID YOU KNOW?

Great Smoky Mountains National Park includes more than a half million acres divided almost evenly between North Carolina and Tennessee.

Junior Rangers

Ready to explore the park?

A great way to do it is to become a Junior Ranger. Pick up the official Junior Ranger booklet (they cost $2.50) at any park visitor center or at the Cades Cove or Elkmont campgrounds.

Complete the activities while you explore the park and then stop by a visitor center to talk to a ranger and get your badge. More than 350 national parks have junior ranger programs (nps.gov/kids/jrRangers.cfm).

You can become a Junior Ranger at Great Smoky Mountains National Park all year, but if you visit during summer, fall, or spring, there are special Junior Ranger programs led by real park rangers. You might learn what it was like for kids to grow up here before computers and cars and to live in the mountains. Check online (nps.gov/grsm/planyourvisit/calendar .htm) or when you arrive at the visitor's center.

There's also an online National Parks Service site for kids called WebRangers (nps.gov/webrangers/) with games and activities, the chance to share pictures, earn rewards, and more.

Are you ready to get started?

What's Cool? Camping in the park! There are 10 campgrounds from which to choose.

SMOKY MOUNTAINS, WORD SCRAMBLE

Can you unscramble these words related to the Smoky Mountains?

YKSMO   _____

GRANER   _____

EKHI   _____

NPCIIC   _____

SRBEA   _____

NTAMIUONS   _____

TIONANAL KPRA   _____

KECEHERO   _____

See page 122 for the answers!

A LOCAL KID SAYS:
"Stop at the visitor center at the national park. They have cool stuff to look at!"
—Emily, 12, Morristown, TN

2

Newfound Gap Road

Tall trees, rushing rivers, and a farm museum

Do you have your seatbelt fastened? Now it's time to put down all your electronic devices and look out the window! US 441, also known as **Newfound Gap Road**, is the only road across Great Smoky Mountains National Park—31 miles from Gatlinburg, Tennessee, to Cherokee, North Carolina. Most visitors to Great Smoky Mountains National Park see the park from this road.

It's a shame more people don't stay awhile! But on this one stretch of road that will take you about an hour to cross, you'll see a lot of what makes the park

A VISITING KID SAYS:
"Spruce Flats Fall Trail was my favorite in the park. We did face painting!"
—Sydney, 11, Fenton, MO

DID YOU KNOW?

Young men built the roads, trails, bridges, and camping and picnic facilities during the 1930s in the Smoky Mountains. This was part of a big government program called the Civilian Conservation Corps (CCC) that was set up during the Great Depression to help families who couldn't find work. Most of the labor was done with hand tools and mules. The young men, who lived in simple barracks, were paid, but were required to send most of the money home to their families.

great—forests, mountains, and wildlife at either end, and old buildings that let you see what life was like for families who lived here a long time ago.

You'll be glad you aren't on a bike! You'll gain 4,000 feet in elevation up into the mountains on this road. Keep your jacket handy for when you stop to check out the views at the top!

If you start your drive at Gatlinburg, as most families do, make your first stop the **Sugarlands Visitor Center** just inside the park. Rangers can answer your questions and you can take the mile-long Fighting Creek Self-Guiding Nature Trail right from behind the visitor center.

A tip: Go to the bathroom when there is one available—like at the visitor center!

Did you know trees tell stories? On the **Fighting Creek Trail**, for example, you can tell you are walking on what once was a cornfield because most of the trees are small. The tulip trees next to the trail are also signs that this was once open ground.

When you get back on the road, watch for the mileposts. They are placed a mile apart and will help you to figure out if you've missed something you wanted to stop and see—such as the **Campbell Overlook** at milepost 3.9 where you can check out the roadside exhibit about the forest patterns and look out at the mountains.

DID YOU KNOW?

Mount Sequoyah was named for the Cherokee who developed a Cherokee alphabet in the 1820s, bringing literacy to the entire Cherokee nation. The alphabet and language are taught today in Cherokee schools. Many other mountains here were named after people who had something to do with the creation of Great Smoky Mountains National Park.

Hungry? You can stop at milepost 6.2 at the Chimneys Picnic Area and have lunch right by the rushing Little Pigeon River. How about a walk afterward on the Cove Hardwood Nature Trail? It's just a mile. Some of the trees along this trail are over 100 feet tall!

If you want a longer hike, try the Alum Cave Trail at milepost 10.4. It's fairly level along a really pretty creek for 2.5 miles each way. Can you hike 5 miles? Remember, it's about the journey—you don't have to go all the way!

Got your camera handy? You'll want it at the Morton Overlook at milepost 14. You can see the Chimney Tops Mountains from here. No worries if you missed it. There are lots of other overlooks along the road—such as the

A VISITING KID SAYS:
"I learned there are only two venomous snakes in this whole area."
—Sam, 11, Harwich, MA

Webb Overlook at milepost 17.7, where you might have a view of the park's highest peak, Clingmans Dome.

You're nearing the end of the road when you get to milepost 29.9 and the Mingus Mill, where you can watch corn being ground!

When you get to the Oconaluftee Visitor Center (almost the end of the road at milepost 30.3), get a post card, write on the back what you liked most along the way, and send it to yourself.

What are you going to say?

A LOCAL KID SAYS:
"I love hiking in the park with my family. It's fun and the views are beautiful!"
—Bentley, 11, Gatlinburg, TN

WHAT'S COOL? Making it up the steep, 2-mile climb to the summit of the Chimney Tops Trail. The reward is the amazing view! (The trailhead is at milepost 8.6 on Newfound Gap Road.)

A Super Trail

Could you hike 2,180 miles? Every year, some 2,000 people try to hike the Appalachian Trail (AppalachianTrail.org) that passes through 14 states and is part of the National Park system. Millions from around the world visit the Appalachian Trail someplace between where it starts in Georgia and ends in Maine, maybe hiking a mile or 2. You could hike part of it in Great Smoky Mountains National Park—it stretches for 72 miles inside the park. Hikers stay in rustic three-sided shelters along the trail, carrying their food. Their packs are heavy! Every year many volunteers work to keep the trail maintained.

It takes about six months to hike the entire trail, starting in Georgia in the spring and ending in Maine in the fall, but only one in four who start make it to the end. Along the way, the hikers adopt nicknames like "Crumb-snatcher" or "Thunder Chicken." What's your trail nickname going to be?

DID YOU KNOW?

At Newfound Gap you'll see hikers with heavy packs on the Appalachian Trail, which crosses the road here. Milepost 14.7 on Newfound Gap Road is the Tennessee–North Carolina state border.

Mountain Farm Museum

No, the log buildings weren't always here at the Mountain Farm Museum located just beyond the Oconaluftee Visitor Center along the river.

They were moved here from what once were other farms in the park so that you can see what life would have been like on a farm here in Appalachia 100 years ago.

This place is a real working farm with vegetables growing in the garden, corn in the fields, and hens, roosters, and hogs on the premises.

Stop in at the Davis House, where volunteers, dressed as they would have been a century ago, help you travel back in time as you look around.

See the chicken house, a sorghum mill for making molasses, a blacksmith's shop for repairing tools, and a springhouse that farmers used the same way we use refrigerators today.

Don't miss the outhouse!

DID YOU KNOW?

There are trees in Great Smoky Mountains National Park that are more than 500 years old.

TELL THE ADULTS

- If you want to stay in Great Smoky Mountains National Park, you're going to need to camp. The kids will think it is a great adventure with streams and nature trails to explore, and, if you are at one of the larger campgrounds, ranger programs to join. There are more than 1,100 sites in 10 developed campgrounds, plus more in the back country. You'll find handicapped-accessible sites if you need them.

- Part of the fun of camping is getting dirty. There are no showers at the campgrounds, though you'll find (cold) running water and flush toilets.

DID YOU KNOW?

The big evergreen shrubs with big leaves that you see all over the Smokies are rhododendron. In summer, some have white flowers, others higher on the ridge have purplish-pink ones.

Some campgrounds are very small—just a dozen sites in the woods. Others, such as Elkmont Campground and Cades Cove, are big and will have more kid-related activities and ranger activities. Cades Cove even has a camp store that sells pizza and ice cream and a bike rental shop. Most campgrounds accommodate pop-up trailers as well as RVs (you can find out more about RVing at gorving.com).

Check ahead to see if the campground where you'd like to stay takes reservations—about half do. To make reservations, visit recreation.gov or call (877) 444-6777.

3

A Roaring Fork and More:
Waterfalls, tall green walls, and rushing streams

See the tall green walls?

Of course when you're driving on the **Roaring Fork Motor Nature Trail,** you will see that they are tall green trees, but they are so big and so dense, they'll seem like a big green wall. The adventure has started almost as soon as you enter the park from Gatlinburg.

Ask your parents to pull over so you can get out and:

- **SMELL** the woods. Does it remind you of anything?

- **FEEL** the soft moss (it's kind of spongy!) and the coolness of the forest air.

- **LISTEN** for birds and the hum of insects. What do you hear?

DID YOU KNOW?

Waterfalls run the fullest after a recent rain. There are so many dramatic waterfalls in Great Smoky Mountains National Park because of all the rain that falls here.

How many different trees can you count? At first, they all may look the same, but look closely and you'll see they are different:

- **BIRCH TREES** have almond-shaped leaves.

- **TULIP TREES** are tall and slim with leaves that are almost square. They sprouted up where open lands that were once farmed here were abandoned.

- **FLOWERING RHODODENDRON** have big, pretty flowers in spring and summer.

- **HEMLOCKS** are evergreens that can grow huge and have leaves that look like brushes.

The hemlock forest, in fact, is one of the several tree communities in the Smoky Mountains. Sadly, they're under attack by a tiny insect and more than half of the park's hemlock trees have died. The National Park Service is working on ways to save the rest.

It's hard to believe now, but this area was once a small farming area called Roaring Fork with a store, a church, and a school. The roads were so bad in those days that people who lived here didn't travel very far. But when the national park was established, they had to sell their land to the government and leave.

If you are up for a walk, you can take the Noah "Bud" Ogle self-guiding nature trail through what once was a mountain farmstead and through the forest.

You might see a pile of rocks where a fireplace once was or an old cabin like

DID YOU KNOW?

More than 85 inches of rain fall in the Smokies' high country. During wet years, some peaks get over 8 feet of rain that ultimately comes down the mountains and creates the waterfalls.

the tiny two-room one where the Bales family lived—imagine nine kids and two parents in that small space. Your bedroom is probably bigger than what the whole family shared. If you visit one of these cabins, don't write anything on the walls. Do your part to preserve these historic places!

Can you hear the Roaring Fork stream? It runs parallel to the road, and it's one of the faster and bigger flowing mountain streams in the park. Don't miss the waterfall here—it's one of the few in the park you can drive to and it's got a great name—The Place of a Thousand Drips.

Do you like that natural air conditioning?

A LOCAL KID SAYS:
"My favorite thing in the park was swimming in the river."
—Riley, 10, Knoxville, TN

What's Cool? The mist produced by waterfalls that you'll feel as you get close—really nice on a hot day!

Ready to get wet?

Take your pick of waterfalls to see in Great Smoky Mountains National Park. There are nearly 20 to choose from! Check them out here at nps.gov/grsm/planyourvisit/waterfalls.htm.

You will need to decide with your family if you want to see one from the road, take an easy walk to one, or hike to one that is more of a challenge.

The national park rangers say easy hikes are short and on trails that can be accomplished without special hiking shoes. Those classified as moderate may be steep in places and the trails won't be as smooth and level. They recommend you have hiking shoes for these more strenuous hikes. Ready to see a waterfall?

- **Laurel Falls (easy):** The trailhead for this hike is 3.8 miles from Sugarlands Visitor Center toward Cades Cove on Little River Road. The waterfall is 80 feet high, but this trail is level.

A LOCAL KID SAYS:
"My favorite thing that I did in the park was hold a water snake."
—Olivia, 9, Maryville, TN

- **Juney Whank Falls Loop (easy):** Follow the signs to Deep Creek Campground. Go past the campground to the trail-head at the end of Deep Creek Road. This hike is less than a mile roundtrip and you can cross the falls on a footbridge! The upper and lower sections of these falls drop 90 feet!

- **Grotto Falls (moderate):** Follow the Historic Nature Trail/Airport Road into the park and take the Roaring Fork Motor Nature Trail to marker 5 at the large parking area. Take the Trillium Gap Trail, which runs behind the 25-foot waterfall. This hike is a more strenuous 2.6 miles round trip.

DID YOU KNOW?

There are large snakes up to 4 feet long that spend most of their time in park streams or along the banks. They are Northern Water Snakes and are not poisonous. Of the more than 20 species of snakes in the park, only 2 are venomous, and the chance of your ever seeing either the northern copperhead or timber rattlesnake is very small.

TELL THE ADULTS

Seeing a roaring waterfall is a high point for many who visit Great Smoky Mountains National Park. Some are large, but there are smaller ones on nearly every river and stream. At one of the visitor centers, pick up the $1 pamphlet, Waterfalls in the Smoky Mountains. You can also order this and others in advance of your trip from the Great Smoky Mountains Association (smokiesinformation.org), which is also an excellent resource for books on the region and the park. Sales benefit the park.

DID YOU KNOW?

The 80-foot Place of a Thousand Drips waterfall at the end of the Roaring Fork Motor Nature Trail seems to disappear when there hasn't been rain in a while.

Hikes to many of the park's waterfalls are moderate, but you can drive to three popular ones:

Meigs Falls: The pull off is off Little River Road 13 miles west of Sugarlands Visitor Center. You likely will miss it if you aren't careful.

The Sinks: The volume of these falls includes the entire flow of Little River. The parking area is along Little River Road, 12 miles west of Sugarlands Visitor Center. Look for signpost 5.

Place of a Thousand Drips: To reach these falls from Gatlinburg, follow the Historic Nature Trail/Airport Road into the park. Take Roaring Fork Motor Nature Trail to Stop 15.

Hiking Safety

Every year, people get hurt hiking to the waterfalls in the park. Be very careful!

Don't climb the rocks near the waterfalls. They are very slippery. Don't try to climb to the top of the waterfalls or swim in the pools at the bottom. That's how people get hurt.

On any hike:

- Stay on established trails at all times.

- Stay with the group. Don't rush ahead or lag behind.

- Carry a whistle (even if you have a phone, reception may be poor or the battery could die).

- If you get separated, "hug a tree" where you are and blow your whistle to alert the adults to your location. Stay there until they return.

DID YOU KNOW?

All animals in Great Smoky Mountains National Park are protected and shouldn't be harmed or harassed in any way.

MATCHING

Do you know your trees? Match the tree to its description!

_____ Birch   _____ Tulip Tree

_____ Rhododendron   _____ Hemlock

A   This tree is slim with almost-square-shaped leaves.
B   This tree is an evergreen that can grow huge and
        has brush-like leaves.
C   This tree has almond-shaped leaves.
D   This tree has big, pretty flowers in spring and
        summer.

See page 122 for the answers!

A LOCAL KID SAYS:
"Leave the wildlife in the park
alone and don't feed the animals!"
—Nevaeh, 10, Morristown, TN

4

Cades Cove: Time Travel, biking, and wildlife

Ready to time travel?

Around Cades Cove you can see what your life would have been like if you had been a pioneer. You can see where families lived, went to church, and worked.

One thing the settlers who followed the Indians here wanted was flat land for farming. That was really important in the mountains! By 1850 there were more than 100 families living here. It was hard work! They had to knock down trees to create clearings where they could plant crops. The men turned those trees into logs to build cabins and barns. They hunted deer and bear and grew corn and wheat. They had horses to pull farm equipment—and

DID YOU KNOW?

Before Cades Cove was part of Great Smoky Mountains National Park, it was a farming community where many families lived. You can visit some of the farm cabins and other historic buildings in this part of the park.

sleds in the winter. The women planted big gardens–beans, peas, potatoes–and preserved food, including vegetables and wild berries, to keep the family from going hungry in the winter. They'd harvest chestnuts to sell. They had to spin their own yarn and weave cloth before they could make clothes. They had no electricity, running water, or phones. The only heat was from the wood stove or fireplace. It would get pretty cold in the winter!

Families had lots of kids who all helped on the farm, but they managed to have time to play too. Ask the rangers what kinds of games kids played.

There weren't roads like today either, just narrow unpaved roads.

They didn't have much money, so they would trade at the store for what they needed—peas or eggs, for example, for coffee or cough syrup, the park historians explain.

This might have been a tiny town by today's standards, but it was considered pretty big back then! There were three different churches, and it was a

big occasion to go visit John P. Cable's water-powered gristmill. You can still see how the mill works today, using water power to grind corn. Do you like cornbread?

While the gristmill was always here, other buildings were brought here, including the blacksmith shop. You might see a blacksmith at work while you visit!

DID YOU KNOW?

Great Smoky Mountains National Park is one of the few parks that doesn't charge admission.

Check out the smokehouse! Since there were no refrigerators, hogs were smoked. Instead of opening the fridge to get some bacon, you'd take a knife and cut some in the smoke house.

The visitor center is in an old log house where you can join some special activities. Get a postcard and write down the most fun thing you have done so far!

You can also check out the old LeQuire Cantilever Barn. The animals had a lot more space than people! Stop in at one of the old cabins, like the John Oliver Place, the Gregg-Cable House, or the Dan Lawson Place. Do you think you would have liked living here?

Where did they all sleep? The parents, babies, and girls slept downstairs; the boys in the loft. Which do you think would be more fun?

DID YOU KNOW?

Smoky Mountain black bears spend much of their time in the trees.

Mornings and evenings are the best times to look for wildlife.

{ **What's Cool?** Horseback riding at the Cades Cove Riding Stables (10018 Campground Dr., Townsend, TN 37882; 865-448-9009; cadescovestables.com)

Take a Hike

There are a lot of trails that start in the cove, including the short Cades Cove Nature Trail and popular 5-mile roundtrip trail to Abrams Falls, which some think is one of the prettiest hikes in the park. Abrams Falls may be only 20 feet high, but it dumps more water than any other park waterfall.

Just finding trailheads like this one can be an adventure! (You can find information and maps for all the official trails in the park at nps.gov/grsm/planyourvisit/maps.htm.)

The Abrams Falls trailhead is 4.8 miles along the one-way Cades Cove Loop Road. You'll want to tell your parents that just after crossing Abrams Creek, you need to turn right on a gravel road and go another 0.5 mile through a grassy field until you reach the parking area. You'll see signs for the trailhead and a wooden footbridge that mark the start. Stop for a selfie at the sign!

Hiking to waterfalls is lots of fun, but be careful! Stay on the trail and don't be tempted to swim. There are very strong currents. Be careful of the slippery rocks!

DID YOU KNOW?

Most of the self-guided nature trails in the park are easy walks, usually less than a mile. Look for pamphlets at the trailhead or visitor centers that will highlight landmarks.

What's in Your Pack?

Whenever you go hiking in the park, the outdoors experts at the Great Smoky Mountains Association say wear quick-dry clothes—if jeans or cotton tee shirts get wet, they'll stay wet and you'll get cold. Make sure you have:

- comfortable hiking shoes or running shoes that have good traction;

- rain gear;

- a whistle in case you get separated on the trail (even if you have a phone, reception may be poor or the battery could die);

- a full water bottle (it's not safe to drink water from the streams);

- high-energy snacks such as power bars, nuts, or dried fruit;

- an extra layer of clothing in case you get cold;

- extra socks in case your feet get wet;

- a trail map;

- a small first aid kit with moleskin (it really helps if you get a blister).

TELL THE ADULTS

There's no better place to start your visit to Great Smoky Mountains National Park than at a visitor center (nps.gov/grsm/planyourvisit/visitorcenters. htm). The kids can get their Junior Ranger booklets, and rangers can suggest kid-friendly hikes and places to picnic. You can get the schedule for kid-friendly, ranger-led activities and buy a guidebook or maybe a book of stories to read around the campfire. Visitor centers also have restrooms! Another good resource for books about the park and the area is the Great Smoky Mountains Association (smokies information.org).

DID YOU KNOW?

Native Americans came to Cades Cove to hunt deer, elk, bison, and bears long before farmers settled here. Cherokees camped and hunted in the Cove for weeks or months at a time.

A LOCAL KID SAYS:
"Bring a pillow when you go camping."
—Kaylee, 11, Mooresburg, TN

Great Smoky Mountains National Park has four staffed visitor centers:

- The Cades Cove Visitor Center, in a log cabin, is in the Cable Mill Area of Cades Cove, near the mid-point of the Cades Cove Loop Road.

- Clingmans Dome Visitor Contact Station is at the Clingmans Dome trailhead, 7 miles off US 441 on Clingmans Dome Road.

- The Sugarlands Visitor Center is 2 miles south of Gatlinburg, Tennessee. Check out the film about the park!

- The Oconaluftee Visitor Center is 2 miles from Cherokee, North Carolina. The museum here tells the story of life on these mountains starting with Native Americans. There is also the adjacent Mountain Farm Museum with historic structures to visit.

Count the Animals

Open fields, like in Cades Cove, offer some of the best chances to see wildlife. While in Cades Cove, you're likely to see:

- white-tailed deer
- black bears
- coyotes
- turkeys
- raccoons
- red fox

Do you have your binoculars?
You don't want to get too close!

DID YOU KNOW?

Mornings and evenings are the best times to look for wildlife.

FILL IN THE BLANKS

Can you fill in the missing spots to spell out wildlife you might find at the Smoky Mountains?

El__   __alamander   __ear

De__r   Co__ote   Tur__ey

Raccoo__   F__x

See page 122 for the answers!

A LOCAL KID SAYS:
"I like to go to Cades Cove.
I always see deer there."
—Haley, 12, Morristown, TN

5
A Big Natural Dome

The Top of Ol' Smoky

What a view!

Congratulations! You've made it to Clingmans Dome, the highest point in the park—6,643 feet above sea level.

And it wasn't even that hard of a hike. That's because you only had to walk 0.5 mile from the parking lot. Sure it's steep, but it's not a difficult trail. It's even paved, and there are benches along the way where you can stop to rest! Imagine if you had to climb from the bottom!

On clear days, you might be able to see five states—all of the Smoky Mountains and beyond—from the observation tower. But be prepared, sometimes the view is covered in fog. Sometimes all you can see are clouds. Sadly, air pollution also can reduce the visibility.

A LOCAL KID SAYS:
"My favorite thing to do is to hike in the forest. I just love to see the amazing plants and animals!"
—Desiree, 10, Gatlinburg, TN

Be sure to keep your rain jacket handy. Not only might it be chilly at the top, but Clingmans Cove gets as much rain as a rain forest.

The Smoky Mountains are part of the Appalachian mountain chain that runs from Alabama into Canada. In fact, if you've ever been to Canada, you might think that the area here seems more like a Canadian forest than the Southeast. The Smokies are also part of the Blue Ridge Mountains that stretch from Georgia to Pennsylvania.

See any flowers? Yellow St. John's wort, pink turtle-head, and small purple-fringed orchids grow here.

What's Cool? Picking wild blackberries and blueberries.

Keep an eye out for the northern flying squirrel, too. If you're lucky, you'll see one gliding from tree to tree using its loose skin like a parachute. However, you're more likely to see red squirrels that the locals call "boomers."

When you look out at all the trees, you may not realize that before this was a national park, many, many trees were cut down to be used for everything from lumber to making paper. The loss of all those trees was part of the motivation to create the national park that would protect the land.

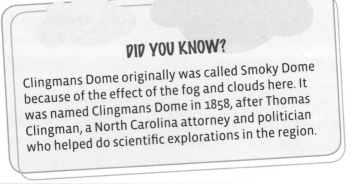

DID YOU KNOW?

Clingmans Dome originally was called Smoky Dome because of the effect of the fog and clouds here. It was named Clingmans Dome in 1858, after Thomas Clingman, a North Carolina attorney and politician who helped do scientific explorations in the region.

The Cherokee who lived here believed bears lived inside Clingmans Dome, and they would have dances here in the fall. There was also an

enchanted lake, they said, that was invisible to humans but where wounded bears could be cured of their injuries. You'll find more Cherokee stories in books at the park's visitor centers.

Ready for another hike? Look for the trailhead for the Forney Ridge Trail— it's just before the path to Clingmans Dome and doesn't require much uphill

trekking—just 3.6 miles round trip. Why not do it? You'll see

weird big circles in some of the rocks around the trailhead. They look like graffiti, but were caused by erosion. In the summer you can pick ripe blackberries and raspberries along the way! Later in the summer you can pick blueberries. Yum!

What's In Your Cooler?

Even if you aren't camping in Great Smoky Mountains National Park, you'll want to bring fixings for a picnic because there aren't a lot of places to buy food.

Help your parents figure out what you'd like to have and try something different, maybe stocking up at a farmer's market. How about:

- tortillas to make sandwich wraps—they're good with honey and bananas!

- carrots, other veggies, and pita bread with hummus

- chunks of cheese, salami, crackers, and freshly baked bread

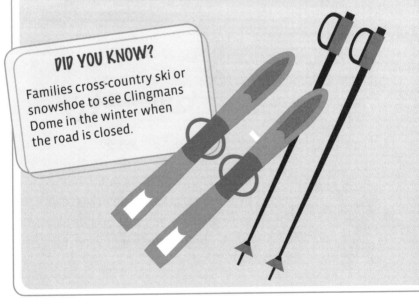

DID YOU KNOW?

Families cross-country ski or snowshoe to see Clingmans Dome in the winter when the road is closed.

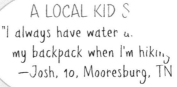
- fruits such as oranges, apples, and frozen grapes that won't get crushed in a backpack

- GORP (good old rasins and peanuts), a high-energy snack that you mix yourself. Make it salty and sweet, crunchy and chewy with your favorite mixture of dried fruits (raisins or dried cherries), nuts (almonds or peanuts), granola, and candy (M&Ms are always good!)

- cookies from a local bakery

What's Cool? Seeing the synchronous fireflies that can light up the night sky in May and June in Great Smoky Mountains National Park. You'll see synchronized flashes of light every few seconds!

TELL THE ADULTS

Be sure to stock up before you enter the park. There aren't a lot of places to get food and supplies inside the park. Fill the car with gas and pack your cooler with picnic fixings (assuming you aren't camping), but also be sure to have the following list suggested by the Great Smoky Mountains Association experts.

- rain gear

- jackets, sweat-shirts, or fleeces for everyone

- a change of clothes for everyone in case someone falls in a stream! It happens.

- sunscreen and insect repellent

- wet wipes and small plastic sandwich bags

- grocery bags to keep trash until you find designated trash cans

> A VISITING KID SAYS:
> "Buy something with a bear as a souvenir to symbolize the Great Smoky Mountains."
> —Ethan, 12, Chattanooga, TN

- binoculars and magnifying glass, great to get an up-close view on a trail

- flashlight and extra batteries in case you are stuck on a trail after dark

- first aid kit

- day pack, including one for each of the kids if you plan on hiking

- filled water bottles and snacks

DID YOU KNOW?

Clingmans Dome is four times higher than the Empire State Building.

Bird Watching

Have your binoculars? Clingmans Cove is a good place to see birds such as:

- common (black) ravens
- dark-eyed juncos with their white tail feathers
- American robins with their orange breasts
- barred owls with their very loud calls
- Canada warblers with their yellow breasts

How many different colored birds have you seen here?

A LOCAL KID SAYS:
"The creeks in the park are super fun to play in."
—Patrick, 11, Knoxville, TN

SMOKY MOUNTAINS WORD SEARCH!

Find and circle the hidden words related to safety!

Jacket   Sunscreen
Bug Spray   Binoculars
First Aid   Flashlight
Batteries   Umbrella

```
J  W  V  B  R  P  X  W  F  N  O  F  F
A  U  S  U  N  S  C  R  E  E  N  N  L
C  F  W  G  R  O  O  A  R  E  K  A  A
K  I  A  S  L  L  E  B  S  B  B  R  S
E  R  N  P  D  I  V  U  T  A  N  I  H
T  S  D  R  E  B  F  M  L  T  C  A  L
E  T  B  A  N  R  J  B  A  T  R  O  I
N  A  T  Y  L  A  N  R  D  E  H  T  G
T  I  I  P  J  R  C  E  Y  R  R  D  H
B  D  R  M  T  Y  K  L  Z  I  X  T  T
Y  F  E  T  U  T  H  L  A  E  N  V  B
B  I  N  O  C  U  L  A  R  S  Q  P  N
```

See page 123 for the answers

6

Cataloochee: Elk, Flowers, Fish, And Forests

Check out the trees up on the ridge!

Have your binoculars? You might see some animals up in the mountains in **Cataloochee**.

Long before settlers found this valley, the Cherokee named this area "Gadalutsi," which means "standing up in a row." They were either talking about all the mountain peaks, some of the most rugged in this part of the country, or the rows of trees on the ridge. Maybe they meant both! Anyway, the name stuck.

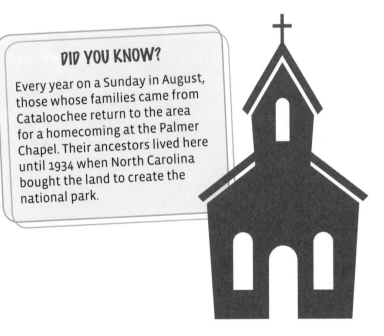

DID YOU KNOW?

Every year on a Sunday in August, those whose families came from Cataloochee return to the area for a homecoming at the Palmer Chapel. Their ancestors lived here until 1934 when North Carolina bought the land to create the national park.

Today it's a great place for your family to hike, camp, fish, and maybe explore a little more settler history.

See how different life was for families just a century ago. Take the Little Cataloochee Trail past some old buildings, including a barn, churches, houses, and the one-room Beech Grove School that older and younger kids would attend together. They'd bring a jar of milk along with sweet potatoes, cornbread, biscuits, and ham in a bucket for lunch, siblings helping their younger sisters and brothers. A lot different than your school lunch time!

You might check out the Woody House. At one point, there were 14 kids living here! It started as a small cabin and expanded. The Woodys welcomed the earliest tourists as a way to make some extra money, feeding them and letting them sleep in their barn. Do you think that would have been fun?

{ **WHAT'S COOL?** Catching "dinner" when you're fishing with your family.

Other families saw the opportunities too, setting up fishing camps and charging fishermen who wanted to fish in their streams. At the beginning of the last century, there were some 200 buildings in this small cove. That all changed when the government bought the land to establish Great Smoky Mountains National Park and the families left.

Today, what once were orchards and farmlands have returned to wilderness where you can enjoy watching the wildlife, especially the elk. Have you ever seen a wild turkey or a skunk? They are here, too.

There are also plenty of places here to picnic and camp. Did you remember your s'mores fixings?

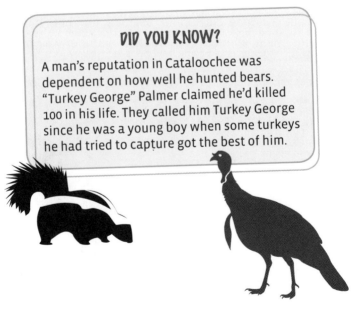

DID YOU KNOW?

A man's reputation in Cataloochee was dependent on how well he hunted bears. "Turkey George" Palmer claimed he'd killed 100 in his life. They called him Turkey George since he was a young boy when some turkeys he had tried to capture got the best of him.

Brake For Elk!

Elk are native to this area but were eliminated in the 1850s by overhunting and the loss of their natural habitat. In 2001 the park began a program to reintroduce the animal to the Smokies, bringing 25 elk here. Now there are at least 125, and the herd can be seen regularly in the fields of Cataloochee Valley. Your parents may have to stop the car to let the elk cross the road.

Elk are huge, even bigger than black bears. An adult male elk—they are known as bulls—weighs 600-700 pounds; females are called cows and average 500 pounds. Check out the male antlers—they can be 5 feet across! In the spring, most elk shed their antlers, which are quickly eaten by other animals. The elk start growing new ones right away.

Never approach an elk or allow it to approach you. Never touch a calf. Even if he seems alone, his mom is nearby. Never feed an elk or any other wild animal.

If you are in the park in the fall, you might hear the male elk make their bugling calls to attract cows. They can be heard a mile away!

Go Fishing

It's about the fishing, not the catching! But hopefully you'll catch something, with more than 300 streams from which to choose. Most people fish for three kinds of trout—brook, rainbow, and brown. Remind your parents to get a fishing license if they are going to fish, but kids don't need one. Cataloochee Creek is a good place for fishing—especially if you are staying at the Cataloochee Campground, as it's right on the creek. There are lots of other good places to fish in the park.

The park fishing experts who wrote the book on the subject (the *Great Smoky Mountains National Park Anglers Companion*) say:

- Fish early in the morning or late in the evening in the larger streams.

- Don't wear bright colors—you don't want the fish to see you!

- Stay low, move slowly, and face upstream.

- Don't let your shadow fall on the water.

- Don't stay in one place too long. Fish a spot for a little while and move on.

Wildflowers!

They are purple and blue, yellow, red, green, pink, and orange.
There are some 1,600 different kinds of flowering plants here.
If you like flowers, you can buy the inexpensive *Great Smoky Mountain Trees & Wildflowers* guide at the visitor center that will fit in your backpack and help you identify the leaves and flowers you see.

Have you seen:

- a yellow black-eyed Susan?

- a white oxeye daisy?

- a blue Virginia bluebell?

- a pink turtlehead?

Keep count of how many different color flowers you've seen!

DID YOU KNOW?

There are more than 20 different purple flowers in Great Smoky Mountains National Park. Have you ever seen spiderwort? It grows to 3 feet tall!

TELL THE ADULTS

In order to enter the beautiful Cataloochee Valley, you need to take a winding, narrow gravel road that has steep drop offs with no guardrails. You may need to stop or back up to allow oncoming motorists to pass.

Along the park roads you may see small signs that say "Quiet Walkway." Pull over if you can and go for a short (less than 0.5 mile) walk into the woods. These tiny trails are a great place to get the kids out of the car—and maybe have a scavenger hunt or play I Spy.

You'll also find 11 self-guided, short nature trails along park roads that are mostly under a mile long and following a loop—easy for kids. Pick up an inexpensive guide at the trailhead or visitor center to the nature trail you intend to take. They're keyed to numbered posts along the way, explaining what you are seeing.

There are also good family hikes here. Don't forget the snacks!

Match the color to the flower by drawing a line!

Black-Eyed Susan   White

Oxeye Daisy   Blue

Virginia Bluebell   Pink

Turtlehead   Yellow

See page 123 for the answers

DID YOU KNOW?

Winter is a good time to spot animals because there are no leaves on the trees. Keep your binoculars handy!

7
Doing Your Part

Got your water bottle?

Be sure to use a reusable water bottle, not a throwaway one. It will become a souvenir once you put some stickers from the national park on it. But more importantly, you'll be helping the environment by creating less trash. Remember it wastes a lot of energy to produce all those bottles and transport them to where you can buy them.

A LOCAL KID SAYS:
"If you are a first-time visitor, go into the park and hike Mount Leconte."
—Sonni Rae, 10, Gatlinburg, TN

Just don't fill your water bottle from any of the park's streams. That water could make you sick because it isn't purified.

National parks, of course, were created to protect the land and all the creatures that live on it. Visiting a national park such as Great Smoky Mountains National Park is a

DID YOU KNOW?
A group of owls is called a parliament.

good place to consider what you can do yourself to help the environment and the animals who call this place home. Talk to the park rangers about what they think kids can do.

That certainly includes leaving what you find—rocks, flowers, leaves. Did you know it's illegal to remove any object at all from a national park? Of course you can take all the photos you want!

Doing your part also includes respecting all the animals that call this national park home, including those

DID YOU KNOW?

If wild animals get used to eating human food when there are a lot of tourists in the summer, they may starve in the winter when it's not available. That's why you shouldn't feed them.

whose species are threatened or endangered. Do you know the difference? A species that is in danger of extinction is endangered, while a threatened species is one that is likely to become endangered unless efforts are made to stop its decline.

Did you know it is against the law to feed the animals? You also aren't supposed to get within 150 feet of elk or deer, and it is a good idea to stay that far from all wildlife.

If you're camping or picnicking, you want to "Leave No Trace." That means you don't want to litter. Be sure to pack out what you have packed in, including all your trash. Keep a couple of extra zip lock bags in your backpack!

If you're staying in a hotel, turn off the air conditioning and lights when you leave. Reuse your towels and take shorter showers to conserve water. That's not so hard! Get out and take a hike or a bike ride instead of driving all day. It's more fun anyway and you might meet some other kids along the way.

A LOCAL KID SAYS:
"If it rains when we're camping, Mom makes us go to a motel."
—Jake, 11, Greeneville, TN

Horse Smarts

The Smokies is a great place to go horseback riding in the mountains. Just remember:

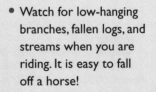

A VISITING KID SAYS:
"Some of the trails and hills are steep in the park!"
—Will, 8, Sarasota, FL

- Horses are big and powerful animals. Be kind to them and respect their strength.

- Know your horse's name and make friends with him.

- Wear boots or shoes with good heels. They should come above your ankle.

- Wear long pants to protect you from getting saddle sores, and a hat to protect you from the sun.

- Listen to what the wranglers say. They know their horses and can best help you.

- Always approach a horse from the front. Don't yell at the horse!

- Watch for low-hanging branches, fallen logs, and streams when you are riding. It is easy to fall off a horse!

Snow Carving 101

The fun in the Smokies doesn't stop in the winter! There's skiing, tubing, cross country skiing, and the chance to carve sculptures out of snow.

Take a big plastic garbage can or large cardboard box and fill it with snow. Stomp down on the snow really hard! Turn your garbage can upside down. (If you've got a box, you can just tear it apart.) Now you've got a block of snow. Let it freeze overnight and you're ready to start carving!

Get out spoons, paint scrapers—whatever you have—and get started. Use a small toy or a picture to guide you.

Snow carvers gather at special competitions all during the winter, but a lot of them started just like you, having fun in the snow.

What's your masterpiece going to look like?

What's Cool? Hunting for animal tracks. Look for them near sources of food or water.

TELL THE ADULTS

There are lots of ways to learn through nature! Besides all of the terrific Ranger Programs at Great Smoky Mountains National Park, The Great Smoky Mountains Institute at Tremont, one of the first environmental education centers in the country to be inside a national park, offers innovative programs that not only engage kids in the nature around them but teach them about the history of the park.

There are kids' summer camps, including Firefly camp for younger kids and others for teens and tweens; a Family Adventure Weekend in the winter; and a 5-night Smoky Mountains Family Camp in the summer with guided hikes, wildlife demonstrations,

A LOCAL KID SAYS:
"I always get pencils from the places I visit. I can use them at school and remember the fun I had!"
—Kadance, 11, Rogersville, TN

sightseeing, and more. During the school year, many school groups come for a nature's classroom–type experience.

There are also day programs that enable families to help with scientific research, such as tagging monarch butterflies in fall, monitoring the park's salamanders in the summer, and banding birds. Call (865) 448-6709 or visit gsmit.org for more information.

What's Cool? Seeing who can spot the most salamanders in your family in one day.

Park Rangers

See the big flat hat? That's the most distinctive part of a national park ranger's uniform. You might meet a ranger in the visitor center or at a campfire program. But you probably didn't realize that rangers wear a lot of different hats— job-wise, anyway.

Some certainly do work on programs for visitors like you. They may also help when there are big crowds in the park. But others provide emergency medical help, patrol the park, enforce park rules, and work on fire crews. They work on the park's websites and are scientists—geologists or biologists, for example.

They also work in big cities at national monuments, like in Washington, DC, and at historic sites all over the country as well as at parks and federal recreation areas. Many have studied something like forestry, zoology, or environmental science in college. Today, no matter what their assignment is, they are all stewards for the national parks.

Say thank you when you meet a ranger!

DID YOU KNOW?

There have been rangers working in the national parks for 100 years.

DRAW A PICTURE!

Make a sketch of an animal track you've seen around the park!

A LOCAL KID SAYS:
"Stop along the way when you
are driving in the park and
look at the views."
—Cody, 11, Greeneville, TN

8

Gatlinburg

It's so hard to choose!

Gatlinburg, Tennessee, has anything and everything you'd want to do—mini-golf and a mountain coaster, tubing and rafting, a zip-line and go-cart track, all the shopping you can want, magic and music shows, even a big aquarium. Check out gatlinburg.com/experience/guides/family.aspx for more information.

Do you like art? This area is famous for crafts. You can see artists at work—sculptors, weavers, carvers—and talk to them about their crafts, which they may have learned from a grandparent or parent, when you visit the **Great Smoky Arts & Crafts Community** along the 8-mile loop trail (gatlinburgcrafts.com). Take the free trolley from

A VISITING KID SAYS:
"I like to walk around downtown and go into all the shops."
—Demetrio, 11, Chattanooga, TN

downtown. Have you ever seen someone make a broom by hand?

Gatlinburg is also the place to souvenir shop. With more than 400 shops just downtown, you have lots of choices besides T-shirts here! Try some good eats and indulge in your favorite treat, maybe homemade fudge or a caramel apple. All you have to do is take a walk along the downtown parkway with more than 200 shops, restaurants, and attractions. Be on the lookout for taffy pulling, caramel apples being dipped, and fudge being made.

DID YOU KNOW?

You can go white-water rafting right near Gatlinburg in the summer with Rafting in the Smokies (813 East Parkway; 865-436-5008; raftingingatlinburg.com) and snow tubing in the winter at Ober Gatlinburg.

While most people visit Gatlinburg in the summer, there's also a lot to do the rest of the year. Check out the gorgeous trees in the fall (how many different color leaves do you see?) or have some fun at one of the fall festivals. In winter, there's a special Winter Magic Trolley to see all the lights, and winter sports as well. Have you ever gone snowshoeing?

The fun continues in Gatlinburg when the sun goes down, too! The performances at **Sweet Fanny Adams Theatre** are guaranteed to make you laugh. Call (865) 436-4038 or visit sweetfannyadams.com to learn more.

Visit **Ober Gatlinburg Ski Area & Amusement Park**, where you can take a ride up the mountain in a cable car,

DID YOU KNOW?

People call the Smokies "Wildflower National Park" because there's nowhere else with so many species of flowering plants.

go ice skating, ride a carousel, play mini golf, and see some critters at a Wildlife Encounter. Visit obergatlinburg.com for all the latest information.

Take the glass elevator up to the Space Needle where you can take in the nighttime view and play laser tag. Or visit Arcadia, the huge arcade.

What are you going to do first?

Eating Smarts

Even if you like chicken fingers and mac and cheese, you don't want to eat it every day on vacation. That's boring. Besides, it's not good for you. Vacation should be a time to try new foods, just like you're trying new experiences. When you are eating in a restaurant:

- Ask if you can order an appetizer or half portion of something rather than something on the kids' menu.

A LOCAL KID SAYS:
"I always like to have breakfast at one of the pancake houses in Gatlinburg. They are all good."
—Gracie, 11, Greeneville, TN

- Split a portion with someone else in the family.

- Drink water rather than soda.

- Opt for fruit as a snack.

- Try some veggies or a salad rather than fries.

Ripley's Believe It or Not

Ripley's Believe It or Not (800 Parkway; 865-436-5096; ripleys.com/gatlinburg) offers hundreds of exhibits about world records in sports, space, animals, and more, plus additional attractions to choose from including a Mirror Maze, an aquarium (check out those penguins), a movie theater, mini golf, and more.

You'll find 500 really weird exhibits from around the world (how about a 12-foot-tall Transformer sculpture made from scrap car parts?); a 5D Moving Theater where you bump, dip, and shake your way through the adventure; two mini-golf courses; and more!

DID YOU KNOW?

Fewer than 4,000 people live in Gatlinburg, but more than 11 million people visit each year on their way to Great Smoky Mountains National Park.

Good Eats

CORNDOGS AND SUBS

For **Fanny Farkles** (656 Parkway, Gatlinburg, TN 37738; 865-436-4057; fanniefarklesgatlinburg.com) calls its big corndogs "Ogle Dogs" and also serves up sausage, subs, shaved ice, and more. You'll love their amusement center, too.

FOR PICNIC FIXINGS

The **Gatlinburg Farmers Market** (849 Glades Rd., Gatlinburg, TN 37738; gatlinburg farmersmarket.com) is open every Saturday from 8:30 to noon from mid-May through mid-October, and is the place for everything, including locally grown produce, homemade cookies and breads, jams, and more. You'll find kids' activities on certain Saturdays along with locally made crafts.

> A VISITING KID SAYS:
> "I like all the shops that sell cool candy in Gatlinburg! Try the candy corn!"
> —Alberto, 12, Chattanooga, TN

FOR BREAKFAST

Flapjack's Pancake Cabin (478 East Parkway, Gatlinburg, TN 37738; 865-430-3966) and Crockett's Breakfast Camp (1103 Parkway, Gatlinburg, TN 37738; 865-325-1403) are great choices.

FOR BARBEQUE

You can't go wrong at either **Bennett's Pit Bar-B-Que**
(714 River Rd., Gatlinburg, TN 37738; 865-436-2400;
bennetts-bbq.com) or Hungry Bear BBQ (490 East Parkway,
Gatlinburg, TN 37738; 865-325-1084).

FOR PIZZA

Big Daddy's Pizzeria (714 River Rd., Gatlinburg, TN 37738;
865-436-5455 and 3053 Parkway, Pigeon Forge, TN 37863;
865-429-7171; bigdaddyspizzeria.net) offers pizza and an arcade!

FOR MEXICAN

No Way Jose's Cantina (555 Parkway,
Gatlinburg, TN 37738; 865-430-5673;
nowayjosescantina.com/locations/Gatlinburg)
also has a Pigeon Forge location (104 Walden's
Main St., Pigeon Forge, TN 37863; 865-429-7779).

FOR A SPECIAL DINNER

Try **Crystelle Creek Restaurant and
Grill** (1654 East Parkway, Gatlinburg, TN
37738; 865-430-1551; crystellecreek.com)
for elegant dining by a creek with a huge
lighted tree and entertainment.

TELL THE ADULTS

There are plenty of fun free or nearly free things to do in Gatlinburg, the gateway to Smoky Mountains National Park, especially with the trolley system that costs just $2 for the whole day. Routes run through downtown Gatlinburg and even along the entire 8-mile Arts & Crafts Community Loop.

- Take a quiet river walk along the Little Pigeon River and stop at one of the pretty gazebos along the way.

- Visit Arrowmont School Of Arts and Crafts (556 Parkway, Gatlinburg, TN 37738; 865-436-5860; arrowmont.org), a national art education center, where you can see an exhibit or perhaps watch an artist at work.

DID YOU KNOW?

Gatlinburg has the world's only Salt and Pepper Shaker Museum (461 Brookside Village Way; 865-430-5515; thesaltandpeppershakermuseum.com), which boasts more than 20,000 sets. Lots of people like to collect salt and pepper shakers.

Go tubing at Greenbrier (greenbrierriver.com), just east of Gatlinburg in Great Smoky Mountains National Park. Greenbrier is famous for its wildflowers and is a good place for a picnic, a hike, or a swim, though the water is cold! The 6-mile, mostly gravel Greenbrier Road starts at Highway 321 about 6 miles east of Gatlinburg. It follows the river past the ranger station, the picnic area, and the Ramsay Cascades trailhead, and dead ends at the Porters Creek trailhead.

{ **What's Cool?** Gatlinburg's midnight Fourth of July Parade.

9

Pigeon Forge

Forty attractions!

No, Pigeon Forge (mypigeonforge.com) isn't a theme park. It's a small town adjacent to Great Smoky Mountains National Park in Tennessee that has a whole lot for you and your family to do, whether you are here for a day or two or an entire week.

Want to be outside? You just have to decide if you'd rather go whitewater rafting, horseback riding, go-carting, or miniature golfing. How about zip-lining? This small town has 30 zip-lines, including some for beginners and canopy tours over the trees. The forests look a lot different up here!

A LOCAL KID SAYS:
"My favorite thing in Pigeon Forge is to ride the bumping river boats. You get to bump into other people and splash them!"
—Skyler, 9, Mooresburg, TN

Of course you can always go for a walk along the **River Walk Trail** (2936 Teaster Ln., Pigeon Forge TN 37863; 865-429-7373) or have a picnic right in one of Pigeon Forge's parks! Maybe you'll catch some music!

There are arcades, laser tag, and **Magic Beyond Belief** (2046 Parkway, Pigeon Forge TN 37863; 865-428-7469; pigeonforgemagic.com), "Pigeon Forge's Best Magic Show."

How about time-traveling back to the Titanic? You can actually experience what it was like to be on the great doomed ship before she sank and view more than 400 artifacts at this museum, called **Titanic** (2134 Parkway, Pigeon Forge, TN 37863; 800-381-7670; titanicpigeonforge.com).

DID YOU KNOW?

The Old Mill has been grinding corn since 1830. Today there's a restaurant here. Try the corn fritters!

Have you always wanted to try skydiving? It's not exactly the real thing, but Flyaway Indoor Skydiving (3106 Parkway, Pigeon Forge, TN 37863; 877-293-0639; flyaway indoorskydiving.com) is a lot of fun, and you'll certainly get a sense of what it would feel like. As long as you weigh at least 40 pounds, you can try it—if your parents let you.

DID YOU KNOW?

The town of Pigeon Forge takes its name from the Little Pigeon River, which got its name from all the pigeons that once roosted on the banks. The Forge part of the name comes from an iron forge built by an early settler.

A VISITING KID SAYS:
"My favorite thing to do in Pigeon Forge is to ride the go-karts with my dad."
—Haley, 10, Mooresburg, TN

Pigeon Forge gets all decked out for the holidays and welcomes anyone and everyone who wants to join the party with trolley tours every night to see the more than five million lights. There are snowflakes and skiing bears and gingerbread men. Winterfest (mypigeonforge.com/events/winterfest) starts in mid-November and continues through February, so no worries if you can't make it over the holidays.

Ready to join the celebrations?

{ **What's Cool?** The Smoky Mountain Alpine Coaster in Pigeon Forge.

Souvenir Smarts

What's in your collection?

Vacation is always a good time to add to one you have or to start a new one. Some suggestions are patches or pins, postcards, bobble dolls—there are so many possibilities.

Towns such as Pigeon Forge are great for souvenir shopping because you have so many choices—more than 300 shops and outlets! That's the good news and the bad news. Now you have to:

- Talk to your parents in advance about how much you can spend on souvenirs. Do you want several small things or one big purchase? Do you have birthday money or allowance you can spend? Some families put loose change in a big jar to save for vacation souvenirs. It can really add up.

- Resist impulse buys!

- Choose something you can't get anywhere else.

A VISITING KID SAYS: "Some of the shops have awesome stuffed animals like bears and deer." —Dalton, 10, Elizabethton, TN

Good Eats

For great burgers and banana splits as well as breakfast, head to **Mel's Diner** (119 Wears Valley Rd., Pigeon Forge, TN 37863; 865-429-2184; melsdinerpf.com).

For old-fashioned southern cooking, you can't go wrong with **Mama's Farmhouse** (208 Pickel St., Pigeon Forge, TN 37863; 865-908-4646; mamasfarmhouse.com), where everything is served family style— breakfast, lunch, and dinner.

Watch the chef dice and slice in front of you at **Little Tokyo Hibachi Grill & Sushi Bar** (2430-212 Teaster Ln., Pigeon Forge, TN 37863; 865-908-0555).

For all you can eat catfish and chicken, **Huck Finn's Catfish, Chicken & Steaks** (3330 Parkway, Pigeon Forge, TN 37863; 865-429-3353; huckfinnsrestaurant.com) is the place to be.

Eat surrounded by country western stars' memorabilia at **Hard Rock Cafe Pigeon Forge** (2050 Parkway, Pigeon Forge, TN 37863; 865-430-7625).

TELL THE ADULTS

You can take your pick of restaurants in Pigeon Forge, but you can also treat the family to something special—a dinner show. Some good ones include:

- **Dolly Parton's Dixie Stampede** (3849 Parkway, Pigeon Forge, TN 37863; 865-453-9473; dixiestampede.com) showcases competitive riding, a chance to meet the stars—the horses—country music, comedy, and a feast with chicken, ribs, corn, and more.

- At **Lumberjack Feud** (2713 Parkway, Pigeon Forge, TN 37863; 865-428-8688) you can be part of the experience as you watch two logging families compete. Watch real lumberjacks at the world's biggest indoor Lumberjack Sports Arena, flying timber dogs, tree climbing, and more. Dinner is chicken, potatoes, biscuits, corn, and more.

DID YOU KNOW?

There is a hotel in Pigeon Forge that stays decorated for Christmas all year long—The Inn at Christmas Place (innatchristmasplace.com).

The Hatfield & McCoy Dinner Show (119 Music Rd., Pigeon Forge, TN 37863; 865-908-7469; hatfieldmccoydinnerfeud.com) the Hatfields and McCoys settle their differences as you enjoy the singing, dancing, stunts, and comedy along with fried chicken, barbeque, and homemade bread.

The Old Mill Restaurant (175 Old Mill Ave., Pigeon Forge, TN 37863; 865-429-3463; old-mill.com) isn't a classic dinner show, but you can eat classic family favorites such as pot roast or chicken-fried steak and pecan pie. See how the pottery and candy are made and watch the corn being ground by the historic mill. This is also a good place to buy homemade jams, jellies, fudge, and more.

Wonder Works

How brave are you? At **Wonder Works** (100 Music Rd., Pigeon Forge, TN 37863; 865-868-1800; wonderworksonline.com/pigeon-forge) you can experience an antigravity chamber, a hurricane hole (65-mile-per-hour winds!), and an earthquake.

They call this place "An Amusement Park for the Mind," and it's chock full of 100 interactive attractions. It's also indoors, so it's a great bet for a rainy day.

A LOCAL KID SAYS: "I like Wonder Works in Pigeon Forge because there is the 360 Bikes exhibit." —Fandy, 10, Bulls Gap, TN

Check out the upside down laboratory, or head to the Physical Challenge Zone, where you can try laying down on a bed of nails. Maybe you'd rather create a version of yourself that walks on four legs! You can also jump from key to key on the giant piano, try on the EVA suit astronauts wear when working outside their spacecraft, or create a masterpiece with the giant version of Lite-Brite in the Imagination Lab. There's even an indoor ropes challenge.

Ready?

SMOKY MOUNTAINS DECODER

Fill in the blanks of the Smoky Mountains–related words to spell out the secret code!

National __ark
W__ld Flowers
Ran__er
Hors__
Sm__ky Mountains
S__ow
Butter__ly
Cades C__ve
Salamande__
__atlinburg
Wat__rfall

— — — — — — — — — —

See page 123 for the answers

DID YOU KNOW?

Kids come from all over the country to play in baseball tournaments at the Ripkin Experience Pigeon Forge.

10

Dollywood

Love them or hate them?

We're talking roller coasters and thrill rides. **Dollywood** (2700 Dollywood Parks Blvd., Pigeon Forge, TN 37863; 865-428-9488; dollywood.com) has plenty if you want a thrill a minute. Check out the Barnstormer, designed to make you feel like you are a daring stunt pilot. You're up 81 feet going fast! How about Daredevil Falls, where you end up in an abandoned logging camp? Get ready to go over a waterfall! There's also Blazing Fury, an indoor coaster where you scream through an old-fashioned town as you try to outrun a fire. See what happens if there is no light at the end of the Mystery Mine coaster.

A LOCAL KID SAYS:
"I like to ride the Wild Eagle because it is fast and fun."
—Samantha, 10, Mooresburg, TN

But you'll have just as much fun if you give the thrill rides a pass. Instead try Demolition Derby bumper cars, the challenge to pull yourself up 25 feet on Lumberjack Lifts, and Sideshow Spin, a junior coaster with plenty of hills and curves. There are lots of attractions to share with younger brothers and sisters and cousins too.

Check out what's playing Live at the Back Porch—you're bound to recognize some of the hit songs! You may also hear music here you don't know as well—gospel songs, for example, or a performance of mountain music by the Smoky Mountain String Band. There's even a Southern Gospel Museum and Hall of Fame here.

At Dollywood's Miss Lillian's Chicken House, "Miss Lillian" serves up some songs with her banjo while you eat fried chicken and biscuits. Ready to sing along?

But Dollywood is more than riding coasters and seeing shows. It's about learning more about this part of the country and the people who lived here in a quieter, gentler time. Visit Craftsman's Valley, where artisans perform the same jobs as they did a century ago. Stop in at the Calico Falls one-room schoolhouse. Maybe you can bring home a wind chime made at the blacksmith shop or dip your own candles with a candle maker. You'll also see woodcarvers, glassblowers, and other artists at work throughout the park.

DID YOU KNOW?

Six of the south's largest festivals take place at Dollywood between March and December every year with special activities and entertainment.

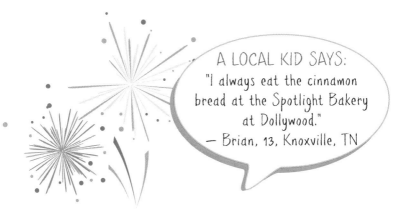

A LOCAL KID SAYS:
"I always eat the cinnamon bread at the Spotlight Bakery at Dollywood."
— Brian, 13, Knoxville, TN

Families come back every year for Dollywood's Smoky Mountain Christmas with four million lights, a special parade, holiday crafts, and, of course, the musical performances. Even the decorated trees get into the act, as every night thousands of lights synchronize with the holiday music.

Whatever time of year you visit, take your pick of souvenirs. How about a personalized baseball bat at The Batter's Box, a glittery rock at the Lucky 7 Mine, or a magic trick from Costner & Sons Magic Shop to try out on your friends?

Stop in at the Sweet Shoppe on Showstreet, where master candymakers show you how they make fudge, brittle, caramel, and all kinds of chocolate treats. Have you ever seen taffy being made? Choose from 60 flavors!

What's your favorite?

Dolly's Splash Country

Dolly's Splash Country might be the most unique water park you've ever seen. It's built into the natural terrain of a 35-acre mountain hollow.

This is the place to ride Tennessee's only water coaster, River-Rush; the multi-mat slide Slick Rock Racer; and the tubing ride SwiftWater Run. If you dare (and you are tall enough), race

> A VISITING KID SAYS:
> "I like the swings ride at Dollywood because they go really high and take your breath away."
> —Madison, 9, Roanoke, VA

your mom or dad down Fire Tower Falls—the twin speed slides. They're 70 feet high! There's a wave pool, lazy river ride, multilevel interactive water play area, and another called Little Creek Falls for younger kids.

Let's all get wet!

Dream Big!

Dolly Parton grew up very poor in a tiny, two-room cabin, the fourth child of 12 with no electricity or running water in the Smoky Mountains. You can visit a replica of her home at Dollywood. But that didn't stop her from dreaming big, and she grew up to become one of the most famous singers, entertainers, and actresses in the world.

Dolly Parton wants kids who visit Dollywood to dream big too. Check out Dollywood's Adventure in Imagination area and the interactive museum Chasing Rainbows, where you can see some of her amazing sparkly gowns, her awards, and even some of her hand-written lyrics.

Do you dream big?

DID YOU KNOW?

Dolly Parton's Imagination Library has given away more than 70 million books to kids in need around the world. She was inspired by her dad, who was very smart but never had the chance to learn how to read.

Bargain Hunting

Sevierville, Tennessee (visitsevierville.com), just 15 minutes from Pigeon Forge and about a half hour from Gatlinburg, is the place to go if you're looking for bargains on anything from running shoes to jeans. You'll even find guitars, banjos, and fiddles at the **Music Outlet** (1050 Winfield Dunn Pkwy; 865-453-1031; www.musicoutlet.net).

There's also the **Tanger Five Oaks Outlet Center** (1645 Parkway; 865-453-1053; tangeroutlet.com/sevierville), flea markets, and specialty stores. You can buy anything from a cast-iron frying pan to supplies for making a quilt or scrapbook.

Did all that shopping make you thirsty? Visit the working **Apple Barn and Cider Mill** (230 Apple Valley Rd.; 865-453-9319; applebarncidermill.com) with its own candy factory.

Ever had fried apples?

A LOCAL KID SAYS:
"Ride the Fire Chaser! It is thrilling and goes very fast and then the ride goes backwards ... awesome!"
—Taylor, 10, Mooresburg, TN

Theme Park Smarts

Theme parks are big, and it's easy to get separated from your family. Here are a few things to consider:

- If you have a phone, make sure you have your parents in your contacts, along with other adults you are traveling with. If you don't have a phone, write down their phone numbers along with the phone number and address of where you are staying on a card and put it in your pocket. Even if you know their numbers, it's easy to get flustered and forget them if you think you are lost!

> A LOCAL KID SAYS:
> "I always carry my phone at Dollywood in case I get separated from my family."
> —Cheyenne, 11, Mooresburg, TN

- If you need help, seek out someone who is wearing a uniform and theme park name tag.

- Don't try to stand on tiptoe to meet a ride's height requirement. Those rules are there to keep you safe.

- Don't try to talk younger siblings or cousins into riding a thrill attraction they aren't ready for.

- No one should ride anything at a theme park they don't want to. Remember, it's supposed to be fun!

If you flew to the Smokies, you probably flew into Knoxville (visitknoxville.com). It's just 35 miles from the park. Even if you drove, it's certainly worth spending some time here. Some places to check out include:

- **The Outdoor Knoxville Adventure Center** at Volunteer Landing along the downtown waterfront is the place to try stand-up paddle boarding or rent a canoe or bikes. It's right along the Tennessee River.

- **The Knoxville Zoo** (3600 Knoxville Zoo Dr., Knoxille TN 37914; 865-637-5331; knoxville-zoo.org) allows you to visit a giraffe, ride a camel, and get face to face with hundreds of animals from around the world.

DID YOU KNOW?

The Knoxville Zoo, just a 45-minute drive from Dollywood, is considered the Red Panda Capital of the World because of its success breeding red pandas. Although they may resemble a raccoon, they are a different species.

- **Ijams Nature Center** (2915 Island Home Ave., Knoxville, TN 37920; 865-577-4717; ijams.org) is a 300-acre nature sanctuary on the banks of the Tennessee River with wildlife viewing areas where you might see owls or other birds, go for a paddle, experience the tree-based zip-line adventure park, or let the kids play in the natural playscape.

- **The East Tennessee History Center** offers interactive exhibits that help visitors understand the history of this region. Kids are admitted free!

- The **WDVX Blue Plate Special** (301 S Gay St., Knoxville, TN; 865-523-7263; wdvx.com/live-shows-schedule/the-blue-plate-special) is a free, live performance radio show that's held Monday through Saturday at noon at the Knoxville Visitor Center.

- **The Knoxville Museum of Art** (1050 Worlds Fair Park Dr, Knoxville, TN 37916; 865-525-6101; knoxart.org) celebrates the artists of East Tennessee and their work. Admission is free and there is a Creative Corner interactive play area for kids.

- **James White's Fort** (205 East Hill Ave., Knoxville, TN 37915; 865-525-6514; jameswhitesfort.org) is considered the birthplace of Knoxville. It is the home of the founder of Knoxville who came here in 1783 and is furnished with original tools and artifacts.

- **The Women's Basketball Hall of Fame** (700 Hall of Fame Dr., Knoxville, TN 37915; wbhof.com) is dedicated to celebrating and preserving the history of women's basketball.

DID YOU KNOW?

Before roads linked cities, and especially in the mountains, people and supplies traveled by railway. You can ride an authentic coal-fired steam train at Dollywood through the foothills of the Great Smoky Mountains.

Dollywood has tons of rides that are lots of fun. Keep track of the rides you went on and the attractions you saw by making a list here!

A LOCAL KID SAYS:
"My family always goes to the Christmas Parade at Dollywood. Sometimes we even see Dolly Parton."
—Hayden, 10, Kingsport, TN

You had such a great time in the Great Smoky Mountains!
Draw some pictures or paste in some photos of your trip!

Answer Keys

Smoky Mountains Word Scramble (p. 11)

1. Smoky
2. Ranger
3. Hike
4. Picnic
5. Bears
6. Mountains
7. National Park
8. Cherokee

Matching (p. 35)

| C. Birch | A. Tulip Tree |
| D. Rhododendron | B. Hemlock |

Fill in the blanks (p. 47)

Elk

Deer

Raccoon

Salamander

Coyote

Fox

Bear

Turkey

Smoky Mountains Word Search (p. 59)

J	W	V	B	R	P	X	W	F	N	O	F	F
A	U	S	U	N	S	C	R	E	E	N	N	L
C	F	W	G	R	O	O	A	R	E	K	A	A
K	I	A	S	L	L	E	B	S	B	B	R	S
E	R	N	P	D	I	V	U	T	A	N	I	H
T	S	D	R	E	B	F	M	L	T	C	A	L
E	T	B	A	N	R	J	B	A	T	R	O	I
N	A	T	Y	L	A	N	R	D	E	H	T	G
T	I	I	P	J	R	C	E	Y	R	R	D	H
B	D	R	M	T	Y	K	L	Z	I	X	T	T
Y	F	E	T	U	T	H	L	A	E	N	V	B
B	I	N	O	C	U	L	A	R	S	Q	P	N

Match the color to the flower (p. 69)

Black Eyed Susan	=	Yellow
Oxeye Daisy	=	White
Virginia Bluebell	=	Blue
Turtlehead	=	Pink

Smoky Mountains secret word decoder (p. 105)
Pigeon Forge

Index